WARBIRDS ILLUSTRATED NO. 25

Cover illustration: Its wings almost obscured by vapour, a Buccaneer of 208 Squadron pulls plenty of 'g' during a mock attack by several aircraft on the RAF base at Waddington in May 1981. Operating from Honington at that time, 208 Squadron transferred to Lossiemouth during the summer of 1983, joining 12 Squadron in the anti-shipping role. (LTP)

1. (Half-title page) Heralding the start of the Battle of Britain air display at RAF Abingdon in September 1981 is this Wessex HAR.2 of 22 Squadron carrying the RAF's ensign on its winch line. The Wessex is one of the two UK-based search-and-rescue (SAR) helicopter types. Six flights of 22 Squadron are deployed around the coast: 'A' Flight at Chivenor, 'B' Flight at Leuchars, 'C' Flight at Valley, 'D' Flight at Leconfield, 'E' Flight at Manston and 'F' Flight at Coltishall. (MJG)

2. (Title spread) This moody view shows a Harrier GR.3, formerly of 1 Squadron, now part of the Harrier Detachment (HARDET) in the Falklands. Note that the outer wing pylons have launch shoes for the AIM-9L Sidewinder AAM. (Richard E. Gardner)

RAF
Air Power
Today

MICHAEL J. GETHING
& LINDSAY T. PEACOCK

ARMS AND ARMOUR PRESS

London—Melbourne—Harrisburg, Pa.—Cape Town

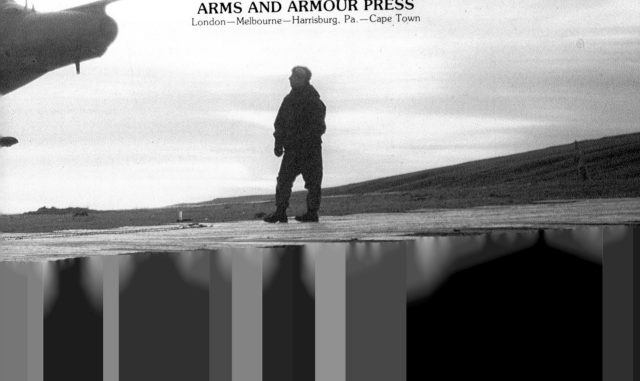

Introduction

Warbirds Illustrated 25: RAF Air Power Today
Published in 1984 by Arms and Armour Press, Lionel Leventhal Limited, 2–6 Hampstead High Street, London NW3 1QQ; 4–12 Tattersalls Lane, Melbourne, Victoria 3000, Australia; Sanso Centre, 8 Adderley Street, P.O. Box 94, Cape Town 8000; Cameron and Kelker Streets, P.O. Box 1831, Harrisburg, Pennsylvania 17105, USA

British Library Cataloguing in Publication Data:
Gething, Michael J.
RAF Air Power Today. – (Warbirds illustrated; 25)
1. Great Britain. *Royal Air Force* – Pictorial works
I. Title   II. Peacock, Lindsay T.
III. Series
358.4 ′00941   UG635.G7
ISBN 0–85368–634–3

Edited by Michael Boxall.
Layout by Roger Chesneau.
Printed and bound in Great Britain by William Clowes Limited, Beccles and London.

◀3
3. Resplendent in the recently introduced two-tone grey overall air-superiority camouflage, this Lightning F.6 carries a practice radar-guided Red Top missile. After more than 20 years of service with the Royal Air Force, the Lightning remains active with two squadrons today, this example being from 5 Squadron at Binbrook.

According to the Defence White Paper 1983, the Royal Air Force musters only 45 front-line squadrons. In 1976, it was recovering from a major cut, not so much in the 'teeth', but in the 'tail'. Today, in the light of the 'Falklands' fallout', some elements of the 'tail' are being restored in a more logical (some would say) manner, the major element on this front being the acquisition of TriStar tanker/transports – VC10 tankers already having been planned prior to the Falklands Campaign.

In terms of combat aircraft we have seen the virtual departure of the Vulcan, always a big hit at airshows, which made its operational debut in the twilight of its career. In its place comes the Tornado GR.1 – MRCA of old – which is now in service with three operational squadrons. Trusty stalwarts in the shape of the Harrier, Jaguar, Buccaneer, Phantom and Lightning remain with us, although successors for some, if not all, of these types are now planned or building. The next generation of V/STOL, or to use the operational acronym STOVL (short take-off, vertical landing), will still be a Harrier, but of a generation spawned in the United States as the AV-8B. The Lightning will eventually give way to the Tornado F.2 air defence variant, while Canberra, Buccaneer and Jaguar will be replaced by Tornado GR.1. The Phantom will remain for a while longer, and to replace attrition some ex-US Navy F-4J Phantoms will enter service next year (1984). Its successor will probably be based on the Anglo-German-Italian Agile Combat Aircraft, although not under the Panavia banner.

The title of this book may well be a contradiction in terms, but the authors felt that the opportunity to collect and illustrate such classic post-war types as the Vulcan, Victor, Hunter and Canberra should not be missed. We have even pulled the Argosy, Chipmunk and Whirlwind into our net. This collection of photographs represents a cross section of units, camouflage and markings carried by the aircraft of the RAF during the period covered. To that end, we have not forgotten the Battle of Britain Memorial Flight, or the ATCs' self-launched glider.

The photographs come from four main sources – the two authors, the RAF itself and industry. Where we have chosen pictures from the latter two categories, it has been with the intention of illustrating the aircraft or markings to advantage, and selecting the best available picture. To those photographers of the RAF and industry whose work we have included we offer our thanks.

While the aviation press, particularly the enthusiast monthlies, will record the various changes as and when they occur, it is seldom that the RAF (or for that matter the Royal Navy or Army) has an opportunity to have its recent past recorded in such a manner. We trust that this volume will add to the collective works of the RAF and its aircraft. We can only hope that the next eight years will be just as interesting.

Michael J. Gething and Lindsay T. Peacock, 1983

▲ 4

▲ 5

◀ 6

4. Training of those aircrews destined for Tornado is, like much of this programme, a multi-national exercise, being conducted by the TTTE (Tri-national Tornado Training Establishment) at RAF Cottesmore. Aircraft from all three key nations – Britain, Italy and West Germany – are stationed at Cottesmore, the example shown here on touch-down being one of the first GR.1s to leave the assembly line at Warton. (LTP)

5. On completion of conversion training at Cottesmore, RAF aircrews proceed to Honington where they join the Tactical Weapons Conversion Unit (TWCU) for specialised tuition in the finer arts of weapons delivery Tornado-style. Here a TWCU Tornado GR.1 'cleans-up' moments after getting airborne from the Honington runway in June 1982. The hardened aircraft shelters visible in the background form part of the 'Gotham City' complex and are used by 9 Squadron. (LTP)

6. Marham in Norfolk was chosen as the second operational base for RAF Tornados and now serves as home for two squadrons, one of these being No. 27, an aircraft from which is seen here on final approach to Greenham Common in July 1983. Another former Vulcan squadron, No. 27 received the Tornado during the first half of 1983. (LTP)

7. The other Tornado squadron now resident at Marham is No. 617, perhaps better known as the 'Dam Busters', aircraft from this unit displaying attractive red and black insignia on nose and tail. (LTP)

8. With a practice bomb dispenser just visible beneath the fuselage, another 9 Squadron Tornado GR.1 taxis for take-off from Honington at the start of a routine training mission in April 1983 shortly before this unit became fully operational. The cut-out on the fuselage just below the cockpit contains one of the Tornado's two integral 20mm Mauser cannon. (LTP)

9. Two Tornado GR.1s of 9 Squadron low-flying over Scotland. The aircraft are each carrying four 1,000lb bombs, two underwing drop tanks and two Sky Shadow ECM pods. (BAe Warton)
10. With four dummy Skyflash air-to-air missiles beneath its belly, the first prototype of the Tornado F.2 air defence variant gets airborne from Farnborough at the start of its display routine at the 1982 SBAC air show. Expected to enter service in the latter half of the eighties, Tornado F.2 will eventually replace most of the Phantoms now assigned to air defence duties in the UK and West Germany. (LTP)

▲11

11. Harrier GR.3s of 1 Squadron exercise regularly in Northern Norway as part of their commitment to the ACE Mobile Force. For these deployments, the dark green of the standard camouflage finish is over-painted in a washable white paint, which is removed on return to the UK. (Rolls-Royce, Leavesden)

12. This Harrier GR.3, assigned to one of the two Harrier units in RAF Germany, 3 Squadron, based at Gutersloh, is seen launching a salvo of SNEB air-to-ground rockets, used for anti-armour operations. This particular aircraft is seen prior to the adoption of wrap-around camouflage in the late 1970s. (BAe Kingston)

13. The other Gutersloh-based Harrier unit is 4 Squadron, also

equipped with the GR.3 version. This quartet of Harriers, equipped with 100-gal drop tanks and twin 30mm Aden cannon underfuselage packs, poses alongside one of the many castles in Southern Germany. Both 3 and 4 Squadrons will receive the Harrier GR.5 (alias the AV-8B) from 1987. (Barry Ellson, RAFG-PR)

14. In support of the British Forces in Belize, four Harrier GR.3s have been deployed there since 1975. Now designated 1417 Flight they are crewed by pilots on rotation from the other squadrons. One of the aircraft is seen returning to its hardened dispersal point. (MoD-Air)

▼12

▲15

15. RAF Wittering serves as the home for the RAF's only Harrier training unit, namely 233 Operational Conversion Unit, which operates a mixture of standard GR.3s and two-seat T.4s, one of the former being depicted here in June 1983. (LTP)

16. This Harrier T.4 shows the latest 'mod' state in 1981 with the Ferranti Laser Ranger and Marked Target Seeker equipment of the GR.3 on its nose, and the radar warning receiver on the top leading edge of the fin and on the tip of the tailboom. This T.4 is assigned to 233 Operational Conversion Unit based at RAF Wittering. (MoD-RepS)

▼16

17▲

17. One of the earliest examples of successful international co-operation, the Jaguar GR.1 presently equips eight front-line squadrons plus a training unit. In the UK, Coltishall serves as the only operational Jaguar base, being home for two strike squadrons and a reconnaissance unit. Jaguars from all three line up on the runway at Coltishall in preparation for a mass launch by sixteen aircraft in April 1983. (LTP)

18▲

18. The gunner's stripe on the fin-tip radar warning receiver equipment and the winged can-opener motif on the intake wall help to identify this Jaguar GR.1 as an aircraft from 6 Squadron at Coltishall. Fitted with a practice bomb carrier on the centre-line stores station, it was photographed on final approach to Coltishall during April 1983. (LTP)

19. Both of the basic Jaguar variants are portrayed in this picture of a formation landing at Coltishall, the aircraft nearest the camera being a GR.1 from 54 Squadron while the farther machine is a T.2 of 41 Squadron. Both of these units are resident at Coltishall although their missions are very different: 54 Squadron undertakes strike duties while 41 Squadron usually confines its activities to reconnaissance with specialised sensors and cameras housed in a distinctive centre-line pod. (LTP)

◀19

▲20 ▼21

22 ▲

23 ▲

20. Participation in joint NATO exercises and competitions is such a common aspect of RAF activity that it is now almost routine. In this photograph, taken during the Tactical Weapons Meet held in July 1980, a Jaguar GR.1 of 31 Squadron emerges from a TAB-V hardened shelter at Ramstein Air Base, West Germany. (LTP)

21. Looking somewhat shabby so far as external finish is concerned, this Jaguar GR.1 wears the coding and insignia of 14 Squadron at Bruggen and, like virtually all RAF Germany aircraft, features instruction and warning notices in both English and German. Noteworthy features are the perforated air brakes and the open gun access hatches. (LTP)

22. Snap! From February to March 1977, RAF Germany had two 20 Squadrons. The outgoing unit was equipped with Harrier GR.3s (and on disbandment these were passed on to 3 and 4 Squadrons); while the incoming 20 Squadron, to be based at 357 Bruggen, was equipped with Jaguar GR.1s. Note the 'wrap-around' camouflage on both aircraft. (Barry Ellson, RAFG-PR)

23. One of the lessons of the Falklands campaign was the need for attack aircraft to have some form of self-defence. One of the options now being implemented is the installation of AIM-9 Sidewinder missiles on the outer pylons of Jaguar GR.1s. This aircraft is serving with 17 Squadron based at Bruggen as part of RAF Germany. (Barry Ellson, RAFG-PR)

15

▲24

24. This view, taken in April 1978, of two Buccaneer S.2B strike aircraft of 15 Squadron, based at Laarbruch as part of RAF Germany, clearly shows the original light grey underside, and the current 'wrap-around' scheme. Also seen here are the 'bulged' bomb-bay fuel tank and the underwing tanks on the inner pylons and CBLS (Carrier, Bombs, Light Stores) units. (Barry Ellson, RAFG-PR)

▼25

25. Stablemate of 15 Squadron at Laarbruch is 16 Squadron, equipped with Buccaneer S.2B strike aircraft. This July 1981 photograph shows an aircraft of 16 Squadron taxying out from its HAS (Hardened Aircraft Shelter) towards the runway. On the outer pylon of the port wing can be seen the ALQ-101D ECM jammer pod, carried as standard fit. (MJG)

26. Bearing faint traces of 208 Squadron's nose insignia, this Buccaneer S.2B now carries the crossed swords and mortar board marking of No. 237 Operational Conversion Unit, a resident of Honington where this aircraft is seen heading for the runway at the start of a routine training sortie. (LTP)

27. This spectacular photograph shows a Buccaneer S.2B of 15 Squadron zooming down the Mosel Valley in June 1983. It is fully-equipped for its war role of interdiction, with the ALQ-

101D ECM pod on the outer port wing pylon, a Pave Spike laser-designator pod on the port inner, a 250-gal fuel tank on the starboard inner pylon and an AIM-9 Sidewinder missile on the starboard outer pylon. At the time of writing, the aircraft of both 15 and 16 Squadrons at Laarbruch are being pooled under 16 Squadron, with a view to 15 (Tornado) Squadron being deployed by the end of 1983, and 16 Squadron handing over the last of its Buccaneers by the end of 1984. (Barry Ellson, RAFG-PR)

▲28

28. Pictured at Scampton on a cold and bright December morning in 1981, this Vulcan was one of a handful of aircraft modified to perform maritime radar reconnaissance duties. Known by the designation B.2(MRR), they were used solely by 27 Squadron and were easily distinguishable by virtue of the fact that they were the only Vulcans to retain a gloss camouflage finish as an anti-corrosion measure. (LTP)

29. The classic delta-wing planform and upper surface camouflage pattern are displayed to advantage in this view of an early-production Vulcan B.2 of No. 230 Operational Conversion Unit at Scampton. Responsible for the training of all Vulcan aircrews for more than 20 years, No. 230 OCU eventually disbanded during 1981 as part of the run-down of the Vulcan force. (LTP)

30. Granted a temporary reprieve from withdrawal by the exigencies of the Falklands conflict, the Vulcan finally made its mark on RAF history with a series of bombing and missile attacks on Port Stanley in 1982. Plans to phase-out the type were already well-advanced at the time of the Argentinian invasion, an event which came too late to save 9 Squadron, one of whose overall-camouflaged B.2s is seen landing at Waddington in May 1981. (LTP)

31. This Vulcan B.2, XM657, seen here in March 1980, was the last aircraft to come off Avro's production line. As illustrated, the aircraft was assigned to 44 Squadron, based at Waddington, and features the all-over camouflage pattern introduced on a number of Vulcans in the latter years of service. To 44 Squadron went the dubious privilege of giving the Vulcan its baptism of fire, when an aircraft of that squadron raided Port Stanley airfield on 1 May 1982. The squadron made five raids over the Falklands during the campaign, code-named 'Black Buck'. It also became the last Vulcan *bomber* squadron in the RAF, disbanding in December 1982. (MoD-Air)

▼29

▲32

32. With everything 'down and out', this Vulcan K.2 of 50 Squadron is seen on final approach to Mildenhall early in the summer of 1983. Instantly recognisable by the rather Heath Robinsonish refuelling drogue fairing at the extreme rear, the K.2 is now the only Vulcan variant used operationally by the RAF, although a couple of B.2s are still engaged in training duties with 50 Squadron. (LTP)

33. The refuelling reference markings, drogue fairing and drogue

are clearly visible in this underside view of a 50 Squadron Vulcan K.2 performing a flypast at Finningley in September 1982. A total of six aircraft were modified to tanker configuration by British Aerospace at Woodford in 1982 when it became apparent that the RAF's Victor tanker fleet was too small to cope with the sudden and dramatic increase in demand for in-flight refuelling support. (LTP)

▼33

34 ▲

35 ▲

36 ▲ 37 ▼

34. Used operationally by 39 Squadron for many years, the Canberra PR.9 photo-reconnaissance variant is still active in very small numbers. Surviving examples now equip No. 1 Photo-Reconnaissance Unit (PRU) at Wyton, this organisation having been established following the disbanding of 39 Squadron in 1982. A PRU example is shown here on take-off. (LTP)

35. One of the more grotesque modifications made to the long-suffering Canberra must surely be that which resulted in the T.17 variant. Engaged on electronic countermeasures and stationed at Wyton, all surviving T.17s are operated by 360 Squadron, unique in being manned by Air Force and Navy personnel reflecting its mission of supporting both services by providing realistic anti-ECM training opportunities. (LTP)

36. The black and yellow undersurface stripes signify that this is a Canberra TT.18 target tug, this distinctive paint scheme having been used by aircraft engaged on this mission since the days of the Second World War. Fin markings consist of a skull and crossbones superimposed upon blue and yellow checks, these indicating assignment to 100 Squadron at Wyton. (LTP)

37. This view of the target-towing Canberra TT.18 shows the underside yellow with black stripes to better advantage, as well as the flight-refuelling target winch and drogue canisters. In 1976, when this photograph was taken, Canberra TT.18s were operated exclusively by 7 Squadron at St. Mawgan. (MJG)

21

▲38

▲39 ▼40

38. Careful study of the two Lightnings seen here at Coningsby reveals several differences in configuration, the most obvious variation being the belly fuel tanks. The aircraft nearest the camera is an F.6 from 5 Squadron, while the second machine is an F.3 of the Lightning Training Flight, both of these units being residents of nearby Binbrook. (LTP)

39. In addition to being a fine interceptor, the Lightning has also earned a more than justified reputation as an air show performer *par excellence*. Seen landing at Greenham Common in July 1983, this Lightning Training Flight F.3 was the display mount for the 1983 season, tragically being lost with its pilot just a few weeks later when it crashed into the sea close to Scarborough's beach. (LTP)

40. Photographs of Lightnings with the highly distinctive overwing ferry tanks attached are rare, but this F.6 of 11 Squadron at Binbrook did appear in such a configuration at Brize Norton during June 1982. The demarcation line between the two shades of grey is also clearly visible. (LTP)

41. Unlike most operational trainer aircraft, the two-seat Lightning was designed with side-by-side crew accommodation, this resulting in a most distinctive bulged cockpit section, shown to advantage in this near head-on view of a Lightning Training Flight T.5 at Binbrook in 1979. Other notable features are the practice Red Top missile and the cranked crew access ladder. (LTP)

42. Just within our time frame (1977), we can depict the RAF Germany-based Lightning F.2A fighters in their upper surface dark green camouflage. This 92 Squadron aircraft is seen here in formation with a Harrier GR.3 of 4 Squadron. The two Germany Lightning F.2A units (19 and 92 Squadrons) were both based at RAF Gutersloh. (Barry Ellson, RAFG-PR)

41▲ 42▼

43. This formation shot, taken in the late 1970s, shows all three current Lightning fighter units in their dark green/dark grey camouflage pattern. Leading the formation is a Lightning T.5 conversion trainer, with Red Top missile training rounds. The upper single-seat F.6 variant belongs to 5 Squadron and also carries Red Top training rounds, while the lower F.6 shows the markings of 11 Squadron. The T.5 variant belongs to the Lightning Training Flight which, together with 5 and 11 Squadrons, is based at Binbrook. (MoD-Air)

▲ 44

▲ 45

▲ 46

44. The second major Phantom variant used by the RAF is the FG.1 which equips two squadrons at Leuchars in Scotland. These former Fleet Air Arm aircraft are also progressively donning an overall grey finish as seen on this example from 43 Squadron in May 1982. (LTP)

45. Caught at the moment of lift-off, and with afterburners blazing, this Phantom FG.1 wears the highly-attractive markings of 111 Squadron, a unit which has thus far resisted the switch to low-visibility insignia. Blue practice Sparrow missiles are carried in the forward fuselage recesses. (LTP)

46. A resident of Coningsby, 29 Squadron is one of two Phantom FGR.2 units engaged in air defence of the United Kingdom. One of their aircraft is shown here returning to the flight-line at its home base in Lincolnshire. AIM-7F Sparrow or Skyflash radar-guided missiles plus AIM-9 Sidewinders are the principal weapons employed although this particular Phantom is totally devoid of armament. (LTP)

47. One of the earliest sightings of a grey RAF Phantom FGR.2, this 56 Squadron example was photographed at Wattisham in April 1980. It is interesting to note that, although it has national insignia of a much reduced size, these are still of the dark blue and red type, the pale blue and pink roundels which are now in vogue making their first appearance soon after. (LTP)

48. Again at Greenham Common in 1983, is this 92 Squadron aircraft still in the green/grey camouflage scheme, which combined with the red and yellow squadron 'chequerboard' markings on the nose and RWR pod on the fin top makes for a colourful aircraft. Sadly, however, these colours will be removed as the aircraft are gradually repainted. (MJG)

49. Responsibility for the training of Phantom aircrews is entrusted to No. 228 Operational Conversion Unit which shares RAF Coningsby with 29 Squadron and the Battle of Britain Memorial Flight. One of their Phantom FGR.2s is shown here in the landing configuration, the unit insignia on the vertical tail being that of No. 64 Shadow Squadron. (LTP)

50. Air defence of the Falkland Islands is in the hands of Phantom FGR.2s of 23 Squadron (formerly aircraft of 29 Squadron). This aircraft on the hardstanding is armed with an underfuselage 20mm Vulcan gun pod, four AIM-9L Sidewinder AAMs on the inner pylons and four Skyflash AAMs under the fuselage. (Richard E. Gardner)

▲51

▲52 ▼53

1. Winner of the Phantom Meet *concours d'élégance* at Greenham Common in 1983 was this Phantom FG.1 (one of the ex-Fleet Air Arm aircraft) of 111 Squadron. It is finished in the current air superiority grey colour scheme, but with non-standard 'D'-type roundels, pre-war rudder fin flash and colourful squadron markings.

2. In distinct contrast, this Phantom FGR.2 of 29 Squadron retains the original camouflage that was applied to RAF aircraft of this type. Also unarmed, it is seen disposing of its braking parachute upon return to Coningsby in July 1981. Note that it still lacks the fin-top RWR fairing which is now fitted to virtually all RAF Phantoms. (LTP)

3. Caught at Alconbury in April 1980 prior to an air combat manoeuvring sortie over the North Sea against F-5E Tiger II 'aggressor' aircraft of the USAF, this Phantom FG.1 of 43 Squadron retains the original finish and colourful markings used by 'The Fighting Cocks' during most of the previous decade. Fin-top Radar Warning Receiver gear is fitted to this aircraft, a practice Sparrow missile also being carried for radar lock-on during the ACM exercise. (P. Foster)

54. Seen against an impressive cloud backdrop, an overall grey Phantom FG.1 of 111 Squadron turns on to final approach at Marham in April 1983. (LTP)

55. Now the RAF's principal air defence fighter, the McDonnell Douglas Phantom FGR.2 variant presently serves with five squadrons in the UK, West Germany and the Falkland Islands. Like many air arms, the RAF has also introduced an overall grey finish on its interceptors in recent years, this often being applied in conjunction with low-visibility unit insignia such as that shown here on a 23 Squadron FGR.2 in 1980. (P. Hatton)

54 ▼

55 ▼

▲ 56

56. Tracing its ancestry back to the Manchester, via the Lancaster and Lincoln bombers, is this Avro Shackleton AEW.2 of 8 Squadron. Based at Lossiemouth, the remaining seven airborne early-warning conversions are close to replacement by the Nimrod AEW.3, an example of which can be seen banking away in the background. (Paul Cullerne, BAe Manchester)

57. One of the more interesting recent developments so far as the tanker force is concerned has been the application of the so-called 'hemp' finish to a number of Victors. Originally adopted by the Nimrod this made its début on the Victor in the spring of 1983 and several aircraft have now been repainted including this 57 Squadron machine. The toning-down effect, however, seems to be somewhat negated by the retention of vivid red dayglo on the hose drum units. (LTP)

58. After several years of service in the bombing role, most of the surviving Handley Page Victor B.2s were modified to serve in the in-flight refuelling role during the course of the early seventies. Now known as K.2s, they feature three refuelling points and equip two squadrons at Marham. In this view of a 55 Squadron aircraft, the dayglo-striped underwing hose drum units are clearly visible, and the belly refuelling point is just discernible. (LTP)

59. Resplendent in its 'bomber' camouflage, a Handley Page Victor K.2 tanker of 57 Squadron, based at Marham, transfers fuel to a Nimrod MR.2(P). This modification, giving the Nimrod an air-to-air refuelling capability ('P' in the designation referring to 'probe'), was made during the Falklands campaign. The fin marking on the Victor tanker is an old squadron design given a new lease of life at the turn of 1982–83. (Paul Cullerne, BAe Manchester)

57▲

58▲ 59▼

◀60
61▲

60. Before the Falklands campaign re-emphasised the flexibility offered by air-to-air refuelling, the RAF had planned an extra squadron of tankers, derived from ex-civil Standard VC.10 and Super VC.10 airliners. This photograph shows the first of the five VC.10 K.2 tankers (ex-Standard VC.10s), which first flew in June 1982. The remaining four Super VC.10s will be designated K.3s. (BAe Filton)

61. The first of the VC.10 K.2s to be handed over to the RAF in the summer of 1983. The aircraft, seen here without its wing-mounted Mk. 32 refuelling pods, is finished in the now-standard 'hemp' camouflage scheme, which has already been introduced on the Nimrods, and is being introduced on the Victor tankers. Note that the rudder is still in the original green/grey colours. A further

12 Super VC.10s (ex-British Airways) are in storage, and may well be converted in due course. The VC.10s were initially planned to support the Tornado F.2s, but with the increased use of Victors during the Falklands campaign, their fatigue life has been reduced, and the VC.10s could be used for other aircraft as well. The VC.10 tanker unit will be 101 Squadron (an ex-Vulcan unit) and will form in 1984. (BAe Filton)

62. During the Falklands conflict of Spring 1982, the RAF modified a number of C-130K Hercules transports to receive air-to-air refuelling. As the conflict went on, a further batch of Hercules were modified as tankers, with the designation Hercules C(K).1. This photo shows one of the pre-release test refuellings (or 'prods' in RAF slang). (Crown Copyright)

62▼

▲ 63

▲ 64

63. Finished in the original white and grey colour scheme, a Nimrod MR.1 settles gently on to the Farnborough runway at the conclusion of its display in September 1976. The massive flap area inherited from the Comet, on which this design was based, is shown to advantage. (LTP)

64. The open weapons-bay doors of this Nimrod MR.1 of 42 Squadron give an idea of this type's load-carrying potential when engaged in anti-submarine warfare. Virtually all Nimrods have now been repainted in the hemp colour scheme and most have also been modified to MR.2 standard, with the relatively new and considerably more capable Searchwater radar. (LTP)

65. This view of a Kinloss-based Nimrod MR.2(P) clearly shows the external signs of the Falklands campaign modifications. The nose-mounted ex-Vulcan refuelling probe gives the type its 'P' designation; the ventral fin was added to balance the probe. Under the wing, on hardpoints originally intended to carry air-to-surface missiles, are two AIM-9 Sidewinder air-to-air missiles, intended for the aircraft's self defence. This particular aircraft is assigned to 120 Squadron. (Paul Cullerne, BAe Manchester)

66. To replace the elderly Shackleton AEW.2s in the airborne early-warning role, eleven Nimrod MR.1 airframes are currently being converted to AEW.3 configuration, with two 180° scan Marconi Avionics radars mounted in the nose and tail. Note also the wingtip-mounted Loral ESM (electronic support measures) pods. The 'hemp' coloured aircraft will begin to replace the Shackletons of 8 Squadron in 1984, when the aircraft will be based at Waddington. (Paul Cullerne, BAe Manchester)

65 ▲ 66 ▼

▲67

67. Another example of 'Falklands fallout' was the procurement in early 1983 of six ex-British Airways TriStar Series 500 aircraft. Four are to be converted as K.1 tanker/passenger aircraft, while the remaining two will be fitted with freight doors as KC.1 tanker/cargo aircraft. It is thought these aircraft will be reformed as 214 Sqn, and operate on the South Atlantic run into the new airport in the Falklands, once it has been built. (Marshalls of Cambridge via MoD/RAF)

▼68

68. RAF tactical airlift requirements are fulfilled by the highly versatile Lockheed C-130 Hercules, the aircraft shown here being a standard C.1 from the Lyneham Tactical Wing which numbers four squadrons in all. Few straight C.1s still exist, most having been fitted with in-flight refuelling probes and redesignated as C.1Ps or 'stretched' to C.3 configuration by Marshalls of Cambridge. (LTP)

69. Pictured at the moment of touch-down, this Hercules has been retro-fitted with an in-flight refuelling probe and is now known as a C.1P. The decision to provide this facility was taken during 1982 so as to permit aerial re-supply of the garrison on the Falkland Islands – the Hercules being the only RAF transport aircraft presently able to land safely at Port Stanley. (LTP)
70. Fitted with new fuselage sections forward and aft of the wing, the stretched Hercules is known in RAF parlance as the C.3, about twenty currently being in service. This example, displayed at the Greenham Common air tattoo in June 1981, lacks the in-flight refuelling probe which is now standard, and was in fact one of the first examples of the C.3 mark to be received by the Lyneham Tactical Wing. (LTP)

71. One of the most attractive colour schemes yet applied to an RAF aircraft must surely be that which adorns 115 Squadron's Andover E.3s. Engaged on calibration duties from their base at Brize Norton, they replaced the Argosy several years ago, approximately half-a-dozen aircraft being modified to perform this somewhat thankless task. (LTP)

72. The last of 56 Argosy C.1 freighters acquired by the RAF and later modified to E.1 standard for use in the calibration role by 115 Squadron, XR143 gets airborne from Brize Norton in January 1978 at the start of the very last operational sortie by an RAF Argosy. Most of the surviving aircraft of this type were broken-up for scrap, but some ended their days on RAF fire dumps and a few, including this one, were sold for civilian use. (LTP)

73. One of the last RAF units to operate the Whirlwind HAR.10 was 84 Squadron, based at Akrotiri, Cyprus. Split into two flights, this 1980 photograph shows the all-yellow search and rescue (SAR) Whirlwinds used on the base. (Rolls-Royce, Leavesden)

▼ 71

▼ 72   73 ▶

▲ 74

▲ 75

74. In conjunction with the Puma, the Westland Wessex HC.2 served for some years as a tactical support helicopter and it is only quite recently that it has been supplanted by the far more capable Boeing Vertol Chinook. Finished in standard tactical battle-dress with black undersides, this HC.2 is from 72 Squadron and was based at Odiham when it was photographed in 1976. (LTP)

75. Following acquisition of the Chinook, a surplus of Wessex HC.2 helicopters permitted several to be reassigned to rescue duties, these eventually replacing the Whirlwind HAR.10 serving with 22 Squadron. Headquartered at Finningley, No. 22 maintains several active detachments at coastal bases in the UK, the example shown serving with 'C' Flight at Valley in August 1979. The winchman, whose job it is to actually effect a rescue, is seen in the open cabin door. (LTP)

76. The Puma HC.1 is the product of the Anglo-French helicopter collaboration deal initiated in the mid 1960s, between Westland and Aérospatiale. The SA330, as it is designated by its designers in France, has proved adaptable and popular world-wide. In RAF service, only two squadrons and the OCU are equipped with the type. Seen here is a Puma HC.1 of 230 Squadron, taking part in the Army Air 82 helicopter championships in July 1982. (MJG)

77. Advanced helicopter training for the RAF is handled by No. 240 Operational Conversion Unit from Odiham, this organisation being equipped with several examples of the two principal tactical support helicopter types, namely the Puma HC.1 and the Chinook·HC.1. One of the former is shown here undergoing repairs in the field, July 1982. (LTP)

▲78

78. The RAF's second type of helicopter assigned to rescue duty is the Sea King HAR.3 which equips 202 Squadron. Like 22 Squadron, this unit has its headquarters at Finningley, maintaining a number of detachments in the UK plus one at Port Stanley in the Falklands. UK-based helicopters are normally finished in a high-visibility yellow colour scheme. For obvious reasons, their counterparts at Stanley differ significantly, being dark grey overall. (LTP)

79. One of the three Sea King HAR.3s, formerly of 'C' Flight, 202 Squadron, but fitted with RWR and cargo-handling gear and deployed to the Falklands in a new low-visibility grey paint scheme. (Richard E. Gardner)

▼79

80. Resident in the UK at Odiham, when this Boeing Vertol Chinook HC.1 was photographed in September 1981, 18 Squadron has recently returned to RAF Germany control, taking up permanent quarters at Gutersloh and operating in support of BAOR troops. This versatile helicopter has significantly enhanced RAF capability in the tactical support role. (LTP)

81. The second Chinook unit in the RAF, 7 Squadron, deployed some of its aircraft south to the Falklands after the end of the conflict. Although now known as 1310 Flight, this aircraft is seen in 7 Squadron markings. The aircraft are crewed by personnel drawn from the UK and Germany squadrons on rotation. (Richard E. Gardner)

81▼

▲82   ▼83

82. Still in limited service with No. 1 Tactical Weapons Unit at Brawdy, the classic Hawker Hunter continues to play an important part in the training of new aircrew although it seems likely that its days are numbered following the acquisition of a substantial quantity of British Aerospace Hawks. Variants presently used by No. 1 TWU are the F.6A, T.7 and FGA.9, an example of the latter being depicted here. (LTP)

83. Among the units still using Hunters in the RAF are the Buccaneer squadrons. As no dual-control Buccaneer exists, Hunter two-seaters are used to train pilots for their instrument ratings. This July 1981 photograph shows a Hunter T.7 of 15 Squadron at its dispersal point in Laarbruch, Germany. (MJG)

84. Apart from advanced flying training, Hawk T.1s are used by the RAF to teach student pilots the basics of weapons training. There are two Tactical Weapons Units (TWUs) doing this job: No. 1 TWU at Brawdy in Wales and No. 2 TWU at Chivenor in North Devon. This photograph shows aircraft of 151 Squadron from No. 2 TWU spelling out their base with their tailcodes. (BAe Kingston)

▲85

▲86

▲87

88 ▶

85. The manoeuvrability of the Hawk has led the RAF to equip 72 of them with AIM-9 Sidewinder missiles for point defence of airfields. Although still in the early stages of conversion the first few have filtered through to the Tactical Weapons Units. This August 1983 photograph shows a Hawk of 151 Squadron, equipped with Sidewinder training rounds. Together with other modifications, involving the fitting of a new compass, strobe lights and a lengthened fairing at the rear of the fin, over the engine exhaust, this variant is designated Hawk T.1A. (MJG)

86. Shadow squadrons active as part of No. 1 TWU at Brawdy are No. 79 and No. 234, a Hawk T.1 bearing the unit insignia of the latter being illustrated here. Although this example is unarmed, the Hawk can operate with gun packs, practice bomb dispensers and SNEB rocket pods, making it a most useful asset in the early stages of weapons training. (LTP)

87. Wearing the black and yellow checks of 63 Shadow Squadron, this British Aerospace Hawk T.1 was actually assigned to No. 1 TWU at Brawdy when photographed in July 1979. Since then, however, a second similar unit has been created at Chivenor, this being known as No. 2 TWU and exercising control over the activities of both 63 and 151 Shadow Squadrons with the Hawk T.1. (LTP)

88. Most famous user of the Hawk T.1 is the RAF's Aerobatic Team, The Red Arrows. In May 1983, the 'Arrows', together with three Tornado GR.1s from the Tornado Weapons Conversion Unit, paid a visit to the United States. This superb formation shot was taken over Great Yarmouth during their pre-visit work-up. (BAe Kingston)

89. ▲89

89. One of the very few Jet Provosts to wear tactical camouflage, this T.4 is utilised by No. 1 Tactical Weapons Unit from Brawdy in the high-speed FAC (Forward Air Control) role over the various bombing, gunnery and rocketry ranges in this fairly sparsely populated area. Unit insignia applied to the aft fuselage is that of 79 Squadron, while the TWU badge also appears on the nose section below the cockpit. (LTP)

90. Used by No. 1 TWU for fighter affiliation work and target towing until 1983, Meteor F(TT).8 VZ467 ended its flying career in the rather attractive colours of 615 (County of Surrey) Auxiliary Air Force Squadron, a unit which operated the Meteor F.8 from Biggin Hill during the fifties. (LTP)

91. Standing out well against an overcast sky, this Hunter T.7 was one of the last of the type to see service with No. 4 Flying Training School at Valley where it is pictured in August 1979. Operating alongside the Hawk for a while, the Hunter was finally withdrawn from the training syllabus at the beginning of the eighties. (LTP)

▲90 ▼91

92. A splendid study of a Hawk T.1 of No. 4 Flying Training School, located at Valley on the Isle of Anglesey, North Wales. The Support Command colours are red, white and light aircraft grey, and the integral windscreen between the student and instructor can be clearly seen. (BAe Kingston)

93. The principal basic jet trainer for more than twenty years, the Jet Provost continues to introduce aspiring pilots to the disciplines of jet-powered flight today and looks like being around for a few more years yet. Featuring unusual dark blue top decking, this T.3 is from No. 7 Flying Training School at Church Fenton, one of three such units still operating this variant. (LTP)

94. The light blue band around the aft fuselage of this Jet Provost T.5A identifies it as being assigned to the Royal Air Force College at Cranwell, one of the longest-lived RAF training establishments. (LTP)

92 ▲

93 ▲ 94 ▼

▲95

95. Flying opportunities for university undergraduates exist at most of the major seats of learning in the United Kingdom, each of the sixteen existing University Air Squadrons operating the Scottish Aviation Bulldog T.1. This example is from the Wales UAS, normally resident at St. Athan. (LTP)

96. The current elementary flying trainer is the Bulldog T.1,

▼96

which also equips the University Air Squadrons. Developed from the Beagle Pup by Scottish Aviation (now part of British Aerospace), the Bulldog has been a successful export for the company. This November 1977 photograph shows two Bulldog T.1s of No. 3 Flying Training School at Leeming, flying over the White Horse on Sutton Bank in Yorkshire. (MoD-Air)

97▲

97. Following the demise of the Vickers Varsity in the early seventies, the Hawker Siddeley Dominie T.1 is now the most senior navigation trainer aircraft in the RAF. All of the twenty aircraft acquired in the mid-sixties remain active today, serving solely with No. 6 Flying Training School at Finningley. Like other training aircraft, they are finished in a predominantly red and white colour scheme. (LTP)

98. Another refugee from Scottish Aviation, originally from the Handley Page stable, is the BAe Jetstream T.1. This December 1976 photograph shows a Jetstream from the Multi-Engined Training Squadron then based at Leeming. The Jetstreams are at present (1983) assigned to No. 6 Flying Training School at Finningley in Yorkshire. (Tony Bobbin, MoD)

98▼

▲99

▲100

99. In addition to about ten aircraft in service with the Flying Selection Squadron at Swinderby, the Chipmunk T.10 is used by no less than a dozen Air Experience Flights whose main objective is to introduce ATC and CCF cadets to the world of flying. Scattered throughout the British Isles, the number of aircraft assigned varies depending on the size of the catchment area, some having as few as two, others as many as seven. This machine is from No. 9 AEF at Finningley. (LTP)

100. This interesting line up shows, from left to right, a Beagle D5/180 Husky – the only one of its type in RAF service – of 5 Air Experience Flight (AEF) at Cambridge, a Chipmunk T.10, also of 5 AEF, and a Bulldog T.1 of the Cambridge University Air Squadron. (RAF Support Command)

101. This formation shot shows the three helicopter types used by No. 2 Flying Training School at Shawbury in June 1978. From left to right they are the Wessex HU.5, Whirlwind HAR.10 and the Gazelle HT.3. The Wessex is an ex-Fleet Air Arm aircraft, as indicated by the overall green camouflage (broken only by dayglo training trim). (MoD-Air)

102. This July 1982 shot shows a Gazelle HT.3 of the helicopter element of Central Flying School, based at Shawbury, taking part in the precision winching event at Army Air 82. The legs resting on the landing skid are *not* those of the pilot, but of the crewman, who was endeavouring to steer a bucket of water on the end of a rope around a slalom course. (MJG)

▲103 ▼104

105 ▲

103. Another type, the Gnat T.1, probably best remembered by virtue of its long association with The Red Arrows, served as the principal advanced jet trainer for many years, only giving way to the Hawk T.1 in the late seventies. Apart from a small number of aircraft assigned to the Central Flying School, most Gnats spent their training careers with No. 4 Flying Training School at Valley in whose markings the example shown here appears. (LTP)

104. One of the newest additions to the RAF inventory is the British Aerospace BAe. 146 which entered service with an evaluation element of No. 240 Operational Conversion Unit at Brize Norton in June 1983. Currently under assessment with a view to possible acquisition by the Queen's Flight in the not-too-distant future, two BAe. 146s are now on charge, being used for communications duties. (LTP)

105. First acquired by the RAF for service as a communications aircraft in 1971, the HS.125 fleet has recently been much enlarged by the addition of four Garrett-engined CC.3s, these joining a similar number of CC.1s and two CC.2s with 32 Squadron at Northolt. Three more CC.3s are presently on order and re-engining of the six older machines is also in hand in order to reduce the nuisance generated by the rather noisy Viper powerplants originally fitted. The example photographed here, on final approach to Northolt, is one of the quartet of CC.1s. (LTP)

106. After operating the original Viper-engined HS.125 for a good number of years, the RAF has recently substantially boosted the size of its communications fleet of these aircraft, acquiring a quartet of Garrett-engined BAe.125 CC.3s for service with 32 Squadron at Northolt. Present plans anticipate the purchase of at least a further three, while the older CC.1s and CC.2s are also being re-engined for reasons of operating economy and to reduce noise nuisance. (LTP)

106 ▼

107. Aircraft of 32 Squadron seldom carry unit insignia so this Andover CC.2 is of particular interest. One of three operated for many years by this VIP transport unit, it was delivered to the RAF in 1965 and has spent almost all of its service career at Northolt. 32 Squadron also has a solitary Andover C.1, finished in a similar colour scheme. (LTP)

108. Seldom seen together except at their home base at Benson, the three Andover CC.2s of the Queen's Flight await their respective passengers at London's Heathrow Airport in August 1975, on what was obviously an extremely busy day for the Royal family. (LTP)

109. Now the oldest aircraft type in the RAF inventory, the de Havilland Devon is still hard at work some 36 years after entering service. All of the dozen or so survivors are assigned to 207 Squadron which is stationed at Northolt and which maintains a small permanent detachment at Wyton for use by personnel of Support Command at nearby Brampton. Pictured at Abingdon in September 1979, this Devon C.2 carries 207 Squadron's crest on the fin. (LTP)

112 ▲

110. The Hunting Percival Pembroke C.1 entered RAF service in 1953 as a light transport and communications aircraft. In 1983, one RAF squadron was still equipped with the type. Based in Wildenrath, 60 Squadron provides communications facilities for RAF Germany. Due to be phased out in the near future, the Pembroke still manages to look smart among the plethora of twin-turboprop and bizjet aircraft used for communication duties by many other air forces. (Barry Ellson, RAFG-PR)

111. The Berlin Control Zone stretches for twenty statute miles in radius from the centre of that divided city. The RAF has the responsibility of providing the visible presence over the zone, and to that end uses two Chipmunk T.10 trainers. The aircraft are located at Gatow, and regularly patrol over all sectors of Berlin,

showing the flag, and simply exercising the right to do so. The Chipmunk itself currently holds the distinction of being the oldest aircraft design remaining in service, having begun its RAF career in 1948. (Barry Ellson, RAFG-PR)

112. For many years, 32 Squadron based at Northolt, flew the Whirlwind HCC.10 on communications duties. This August 1977 photograph shows one of the squadron's Whirlwinds over Tower Bridge in London. The Whirlwind has now given way to the Gazelle. (MoD-RepS)

113. Maintained in immaculate condition and finished in a basically red and dark-blue colour scheme, this Wessex HCC.4 is one of two assigned to the Queen's Flight at Benson, originally having been taken on charge during the course of 1969. (LTP)

113 ▼

▲114

114. Looking extremely smart in a grey and white VIP-type colour scheme, this Gazelle HT.3 is one of two presently operated by 32 Squadron on routine communications duties. No. 32's first Gazelle, an HCC.4, was handed over in the late seventies and was initially used alongside the Westland Whirlwind, the latter type being retired in 1980. (LTP)

115. Although the RAF Regiment man the Rapier point-defence missile defences of RAF airfields, the layered medium SAM defences, in the form of the Bloodhound II, are the responsibility of the RAF proper. This July 1981 photograph shows the Bloodhounds of 'C' Flight, 25 Squadron at Laarbruch. All RAF Germany-based Bloodhounds have been withdrawn to the United Kingdom, and this unit now defends an area of East Anglia. (MJG)

▼115

116. The Air Training Corps, besides having access to Chipmunks for air experience flying, has a thriving glider element. As the old Sedburghs and Kirby Cadet Mk.3s gradually retire, the new motor-glider takes their place. Some 40 Slingsby Venture T.2 and T.3 motor-gliders have been procured. Instead of being winched into the air (or even given an aero-tow) the Venture has its own powerplant, like a light aircraft, and flies into the air. Once at the required altitude, the motor is stopped and the unpowered gliding begins. This photo shows the Venture T.2. (HQ Air Cadets)

117. At the high performance end of ATC gliding, the organisation received a boost in September 1983 with the handing over of the first of ten ASK 21 Vanguard two-seat gliders (two of which are illustrated) and five ASW 19 Valiant single-seaters. These gliders will replace the Swallow, used to give instructors advanced experience. (HQ Air Cadets)

117▼

118. The reputation of The Red Arrows as the world's premier aerobatic team was secured during the late 1960s and early 1970s, when the team flew the Gnat T.1. This photograph shows the team making a diamond-nine pass at an air show during the late 1970s. (MJG)

119. Pictured heading for dispersal upon arrival at Coningsby in July 1979, The Red Arrows used the Gnat T.1 as their display mount until the end of the 1979 season, converting to the British Aerospace Hawk T.1 during the ensuing winter. (LTP)

▲120

▲121

120. No pictorial survey of the Royal Air Force would be complete without at least one illustration of the Battle of Britain Memorial Flight. In this photograph, taken during the summer of 1983, the last Hurricane to be built formates with a Spitfire V and the last airworthy Lancaster bomber. (LTP)

121. Tornado tailpiece. This unusual tail-on shot of a 617 Squadron Tornado GR.1 in a hardened aircraft shelter at Honington, shows to effect the under-surface camouflage. Note that the aircraft serial number of the Tornado is located underneath the stabilator, and not in the usual position under the wings. Notice, too, the extended airbrakes on each side of the fin. (MoD-RepS)